W.O.W.

CHRISTMAS

SONGBOOK

30 TOP CHRISTIAN ARTISTS AND HOLIDAY SONGS

WOW CHRISTMAS (GREEN) recorded on Word CD #080688 641429

Edited by

BRYCE INMAN & KEN BARKER

Transcribed by

BRYCE INMAN, BILL WOLAVER & DANNY ZALOUDIK

WORD MUSIC®

WOW CHRISTMAS

SONGBOOK

30 TOP CHRISTIAN ARTISTS AND HOLIDAY SONGS

WOW CHRISTMAS (GREEN)

CONTENTS

A Christmas to Remember

Recorded by Amy Grant

Words and Music by
**AMY GRANT, BEVERLY DARNALL
and CHRIS EATON**

to re - mem - ber.

Joy to the World

Recorded by Natalie Grant

ISAAC WATTS

GEORGE FREDERICK HANDEL
Arranged by Bernie Herms

Hark! the Herald Angels Sing

Recorded by Rebecca St. James

CHARLES WESLEY

FELIX MENDELSSOHN
*Arranged by Rebecca St. James
and Matt Bronleewe*

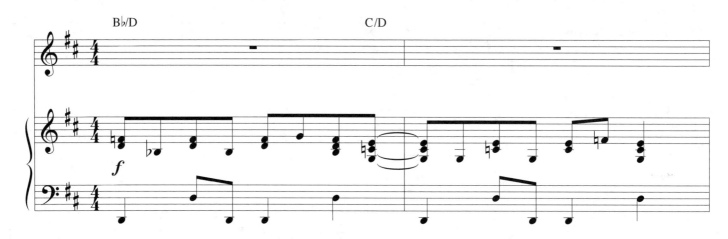

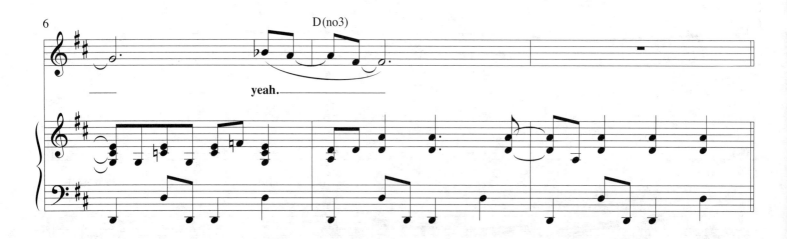

O Little Town of Bethlehem

Recorded by Steven Curtis Chapman

PHILLIPS BROOKS

LEWIS H. REDNER
Arranged by Steven Curtis Chapman

1. O lit - tle town of Beth - le - hem, how still we see thee lie!
(2.) Christ is born of Ma - ry, and gath - ered all a - bove.
(3.) ho - ly Child of Beth - le - hem! De - scend to us, we pray;

O Come, All Ye Faithful

Recorded by TobyMac

Latin Hymn, ascribed to J. F. Wade

JOHN FRANCIS WADE
Arranged by Toby McKeehan and Dave Clo

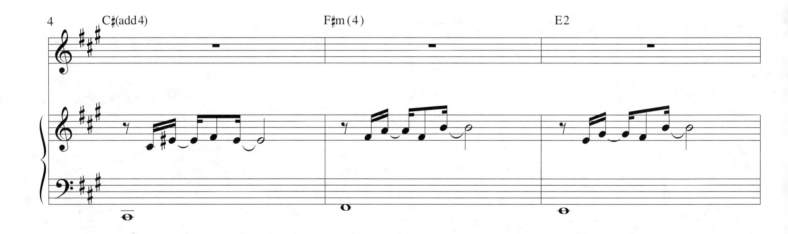

O come, all ye

What Child Is This?

Recorded by ZOEgirl

WILLIAM C. DIX

Traditional English melody

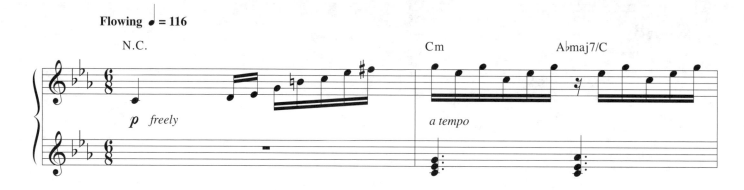

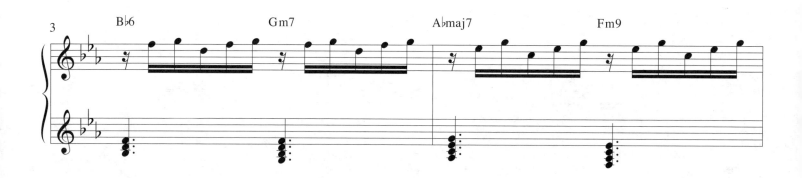

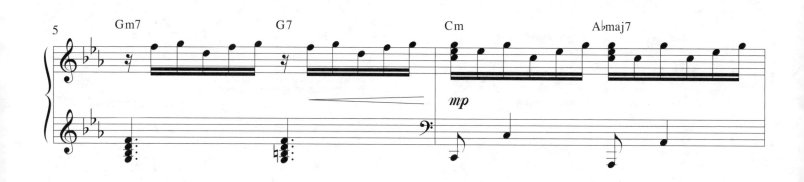

The Christmas Shoes

Recorded by Newsong

**Words and Music by
EDDIE CARSWELL and
LEONARD AHLSTROM**

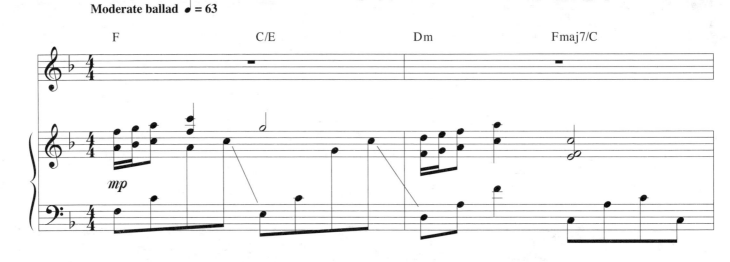

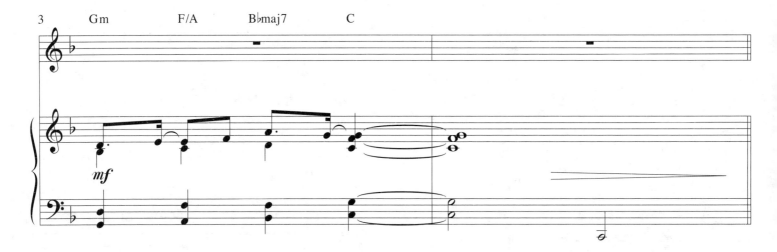

It was al-most Christ-mas time.___ There I stood in an-oth-er line___

night.   I want her to— look beau - ti - ful— if

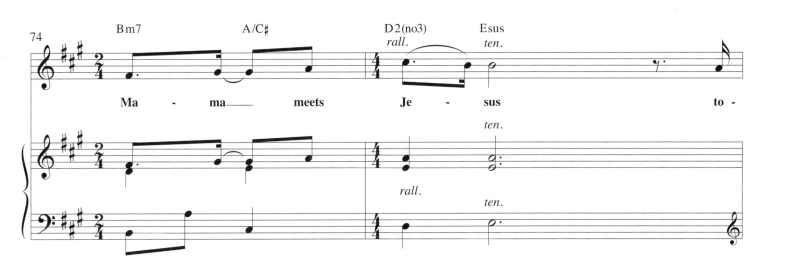

Ma - ma— meets Je - sus   to -

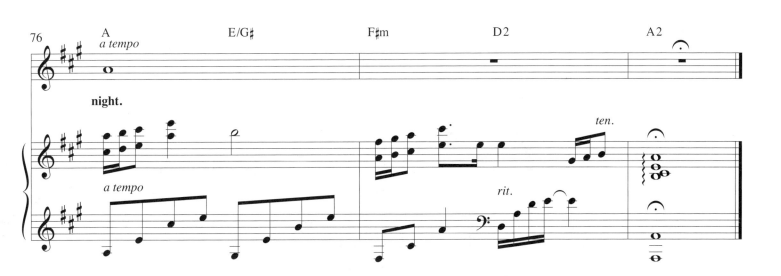

night.

I'll Be Home for Christmas

Recorded by Jaci Velasquez

**Words and Music by
KIM GANNON and
WALTER KENT**

Freely, with much feeling

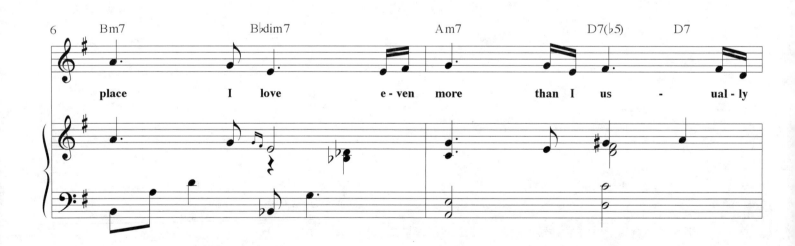

dreams.

Angels We Have Heard on High

Recorded by Chris Tomlin

Traditional French Carol
Arranged by Ed Cash and Chris Tomlin

Moderately ♩ = 88

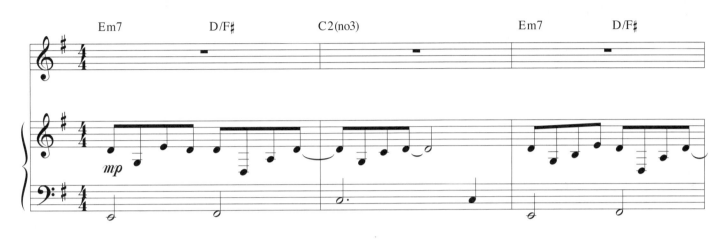

1. An - gels we have heard on high,
2. Shep - herds, why this ju - bi - lee?

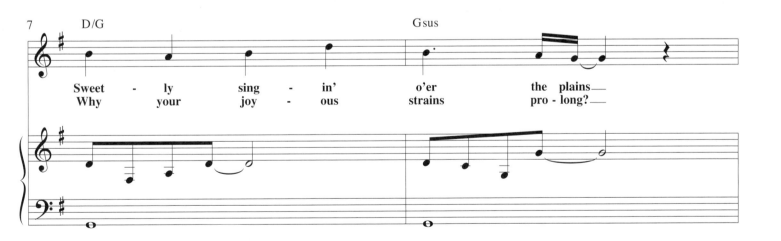

Sweet - ly sing - in' o'er the plains
Why your joy - ous strains pro - long?

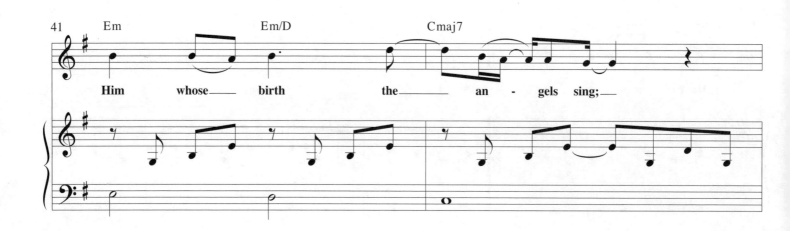

72

Little Drummer Boy

Recorded by Jars of Clay

Words and Music by
KATHERINE DAVIS, HENRY ONORATI
and HARRY SIMEONE

when_____ we_____ come.

Lit - tle Ba - by, Pa -

rum - pum - pum - pum,

Away in a Manger

Recorded by Casting Crowns

Source Unknown, stanzas 1, 2
JOHN T. McFARLAND, stanza 3

JAMES R. MURRAY
and WILLIAM J. KIRKPATRICK
Arranged by Dale Oliver

O Come, O Come, Emmanual

Recorded by Third Day

Latin hymn

Adapted from Plainsong by Thomas Helmore
Arranged by Scotty Wilbanks, Mac Powell, Mark Lee,
Tai Anderson, Brad Avery and David Carr

O Holy Night

Recorded by BarlowGirl

JOHN S. DWIGHT

ADOLPHE ADAM
Arranged by Otto Price

Don't Save It All for Christmas Day

Recorded by Avalon

**Words and Music by
PETER ZIZZO, RIC WAKE
and CELINE DION**

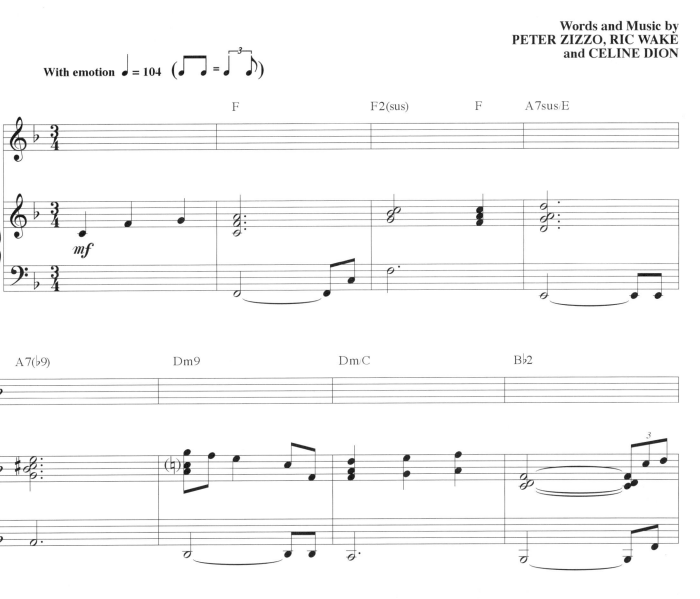

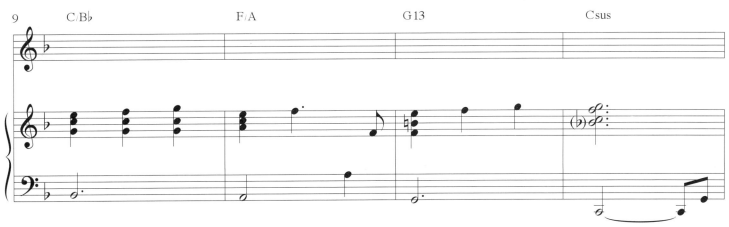

We Wish You a Merry Christmas

Recorded by CeCe Winans

Traditional

We wish you a Mer - ry —— Christ -

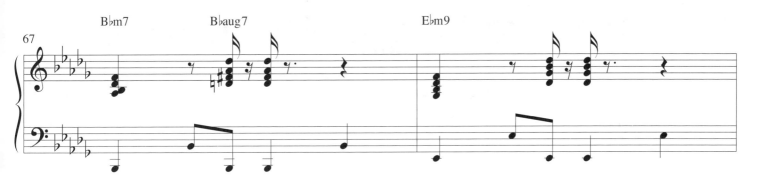

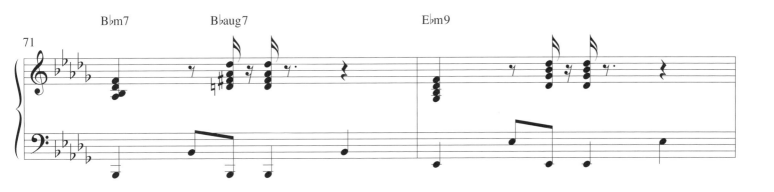

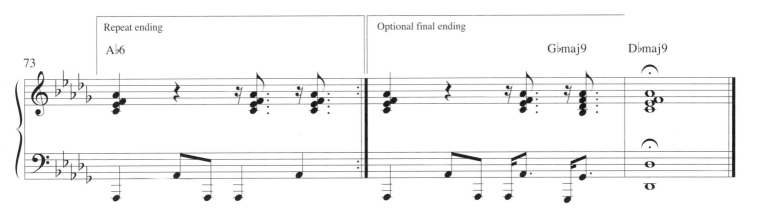

Have Yourself a Merry Little Christmas

Recorded by Joy Williams

**Words and Music by
HUGH MARTIN
and RALPH BLANE**
Arranged by Carl Marsh

From now on our trou - bles_____ will be miles a -

way._____ Here we are as in

old - en days,_____ hap - py_____ gol - den days of

yore,_____ faith - ful friends who are

God Rest Ye Merry, Gentlemen

Recorded by Bethany Dillon

OLD ENGLISH CAROL
Arranged by Ed Cash

Welcome to Our World

Recorded by Michael W. Smith

**Words and Music by
CHRIS RICE**

Somewhat rubato, with much expression ♩ = 76

Let It Snow, Let It Snow, Let It Snow

Recorded by Matthew West

**Words and Music by
SAMMY CAHN
and JULE STYNE**

Mary, Did You Know?

Recorded by Clay Aiken

**Words and Music by
MARK LOWRY and
BUDDY GREENE**

1. Ma - ry, did you

Jingle Bell Rock

Recorded by Point of Grace

**Words and Music by
JOE BEAL and
JIM BOOTHE**

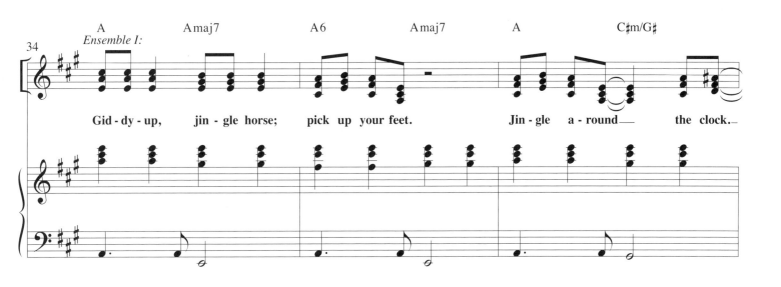

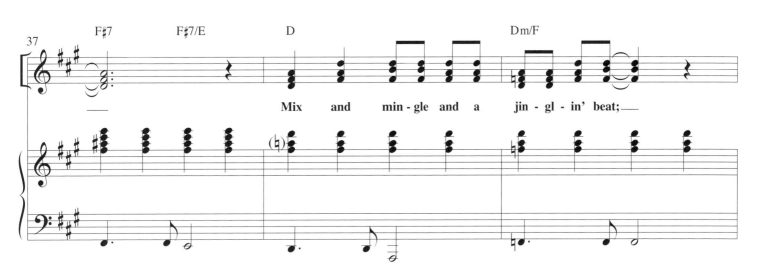

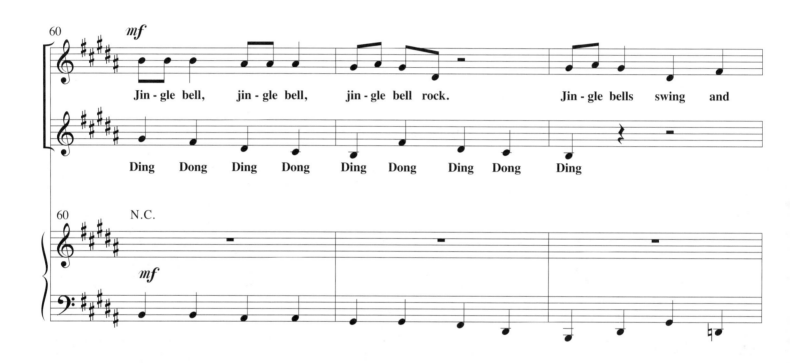

We Three Kings

Recorded by Building 429

Words and Music by
JOHN H. HOPKINS, JR.
Arranged by Jason Roy and Jesse Garcia

Rhythmically ♪ = 158

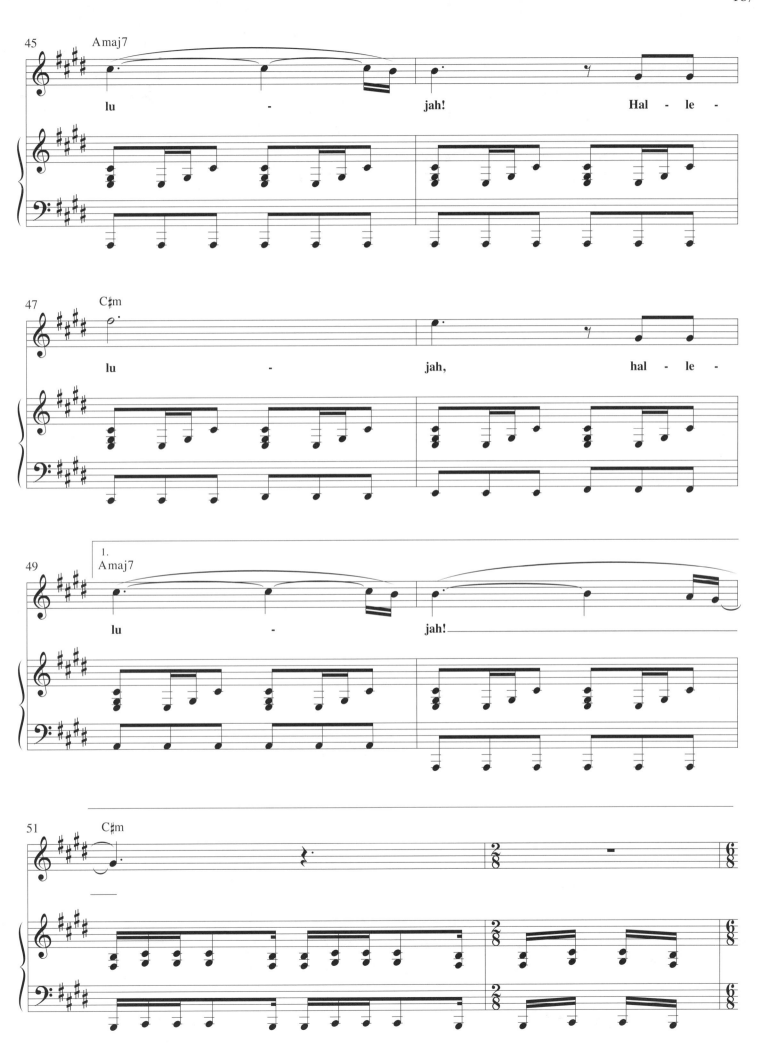

It Came upon the Midnight Clear

Recorded by Kutless

EDMUND H. SEARS

RICHARD S. WILLIS
*Arranged by Micah Sumrall, Aaron Sprinkle
and Larz Katz Gaarde*

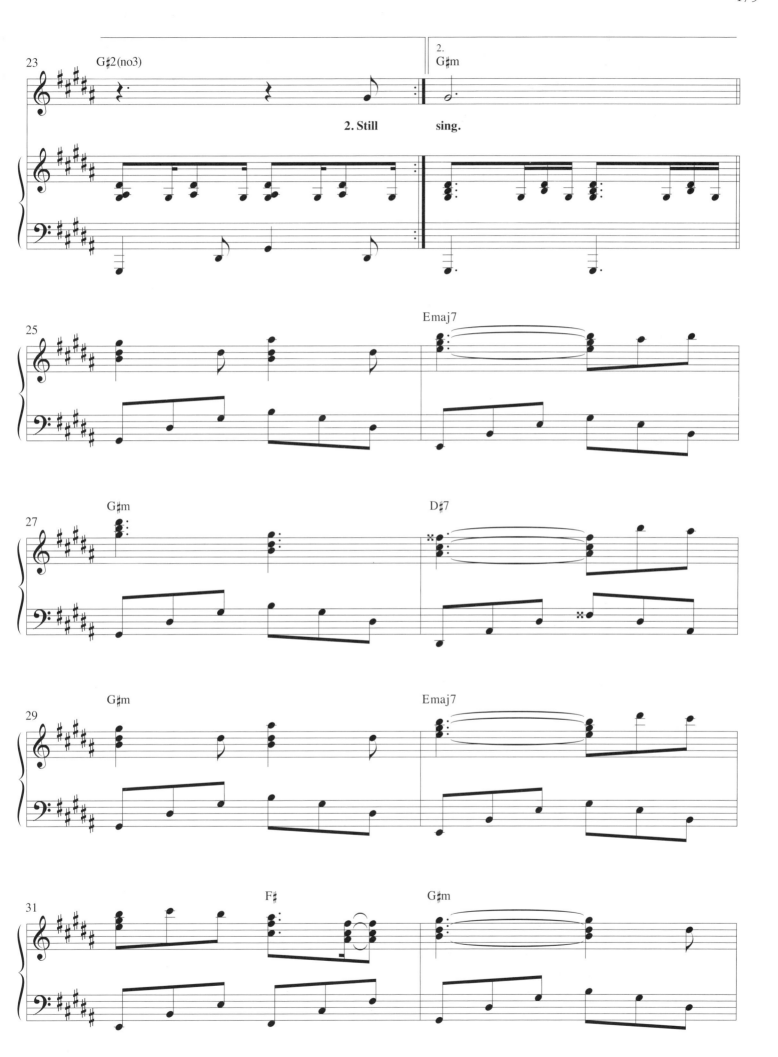

Deck the Halls

Recorded by Relient K

Old Welsh Air
Arranged by Matt Thiessen

EVEN IF YOU POSSESS A **CCLI** LICENSE YOU CANNOT COPY ANY MUSIC FROM THIS BOOK.
If you have questions about CCLI, please call 800/234-2446.

Go, Tell It on the Mountain

Recorded by Big Daddy Weave

Traditional Spiritual
*Arranged by Mike Weaver
and Jeremy Redmon*

shone a ho - ly_____ light._____

2. The shep - herds feared and_____
3. in a low - ly_____

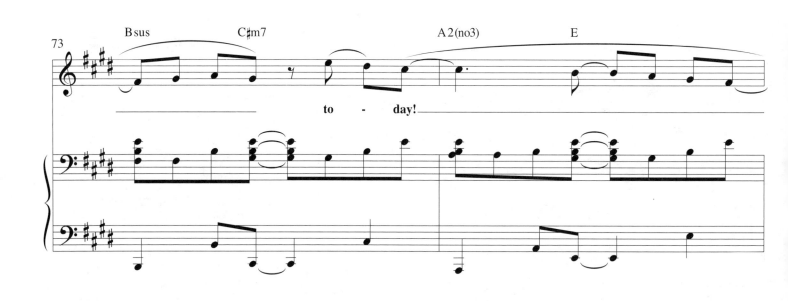

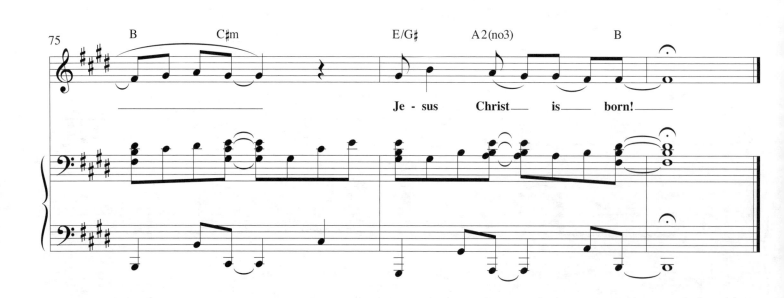

Silent Night

Recorded by Selah

JOSEPH MOHR

FRANZ GRUBER
*Arranged by Nicol Smith, Todd Smith,
Allan Hall and Michael Omartian*

Gently, with some freedom ♩ = 84

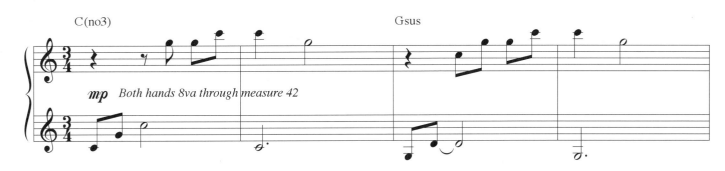

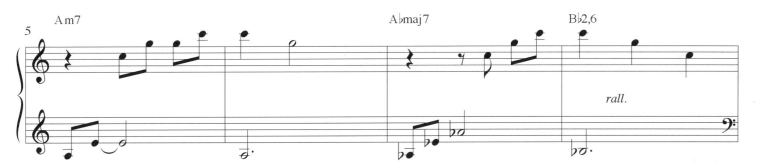

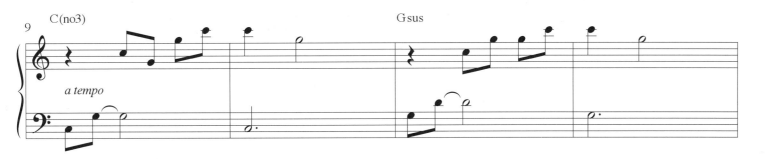

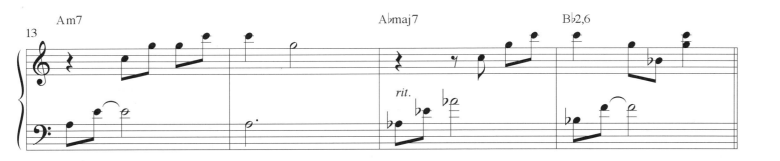

192

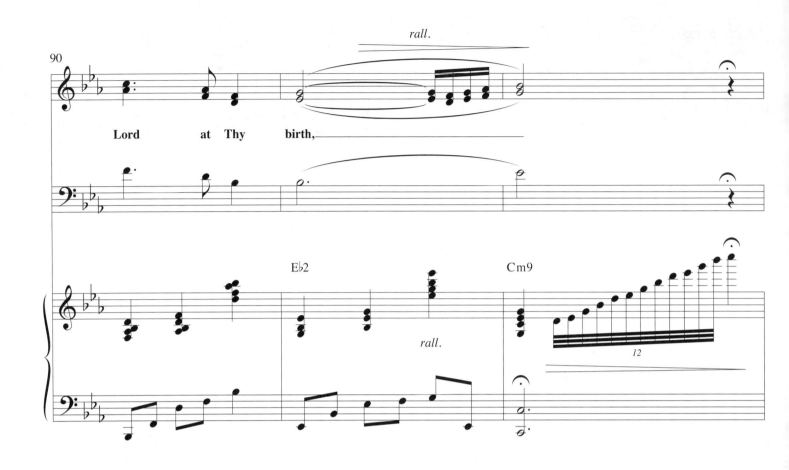

Lord at Thy birth,

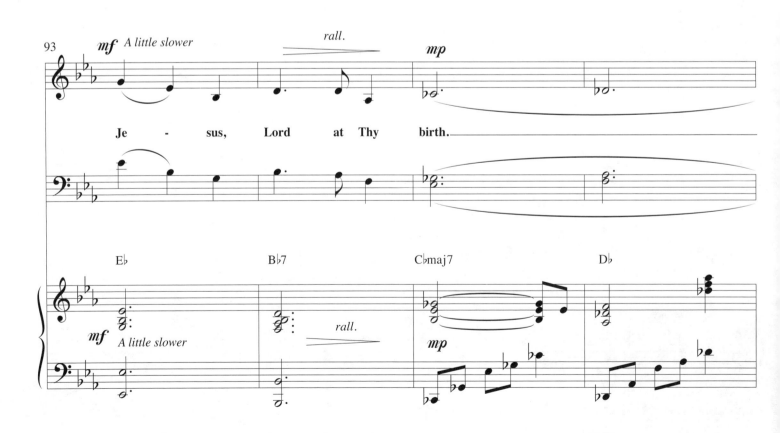

Je - sus, Lord at Thy birth.

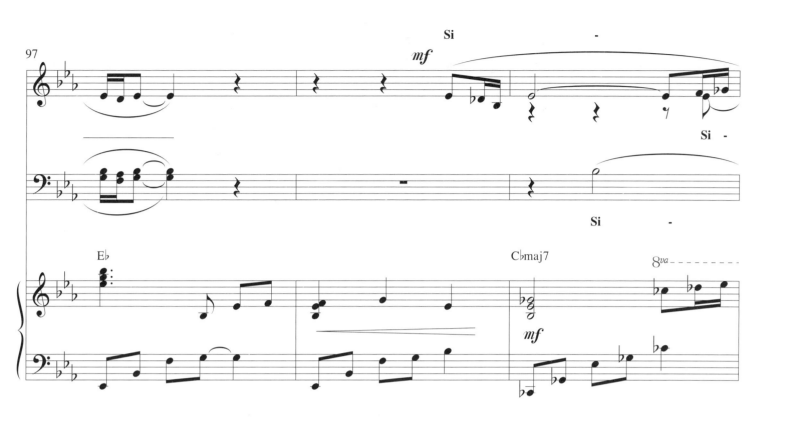

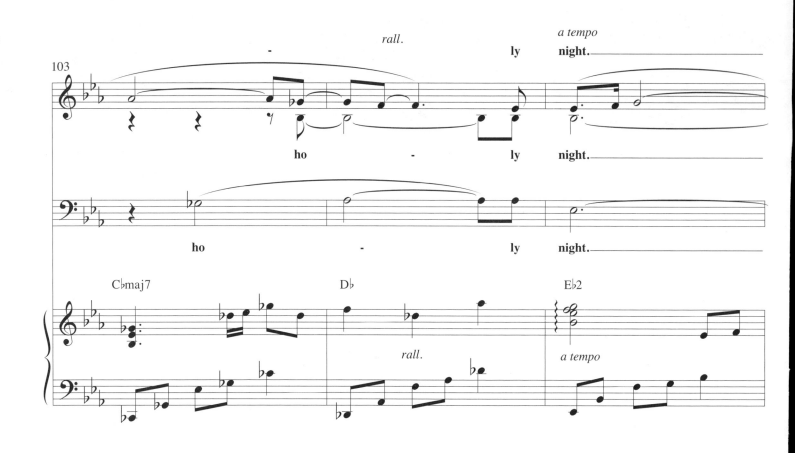

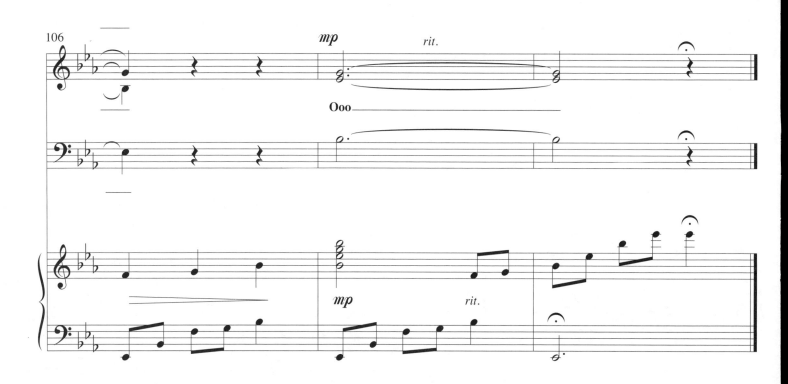

Feliz Navidad

Recorded by David Crowder Band

Words and Music by
JOSE FELICIANO

Happy latin feel ♩ = 138

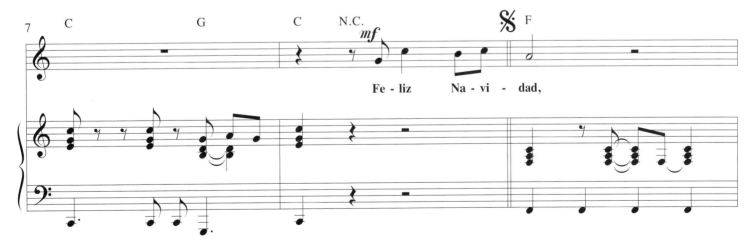

Fe - liz Na - vi - dad,

The First Noel

Recorded by Mark Schultz

Traditional English Carol

W. Sandys' *Christmas Carols*
Arranged by Mark Schultz
and Brown Bannister

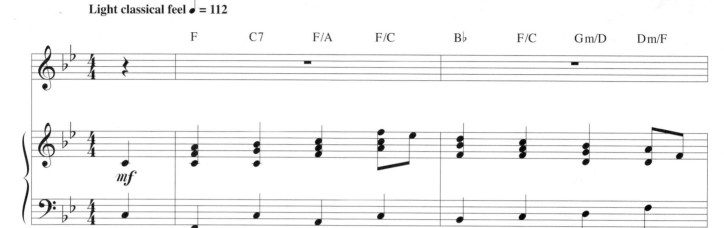

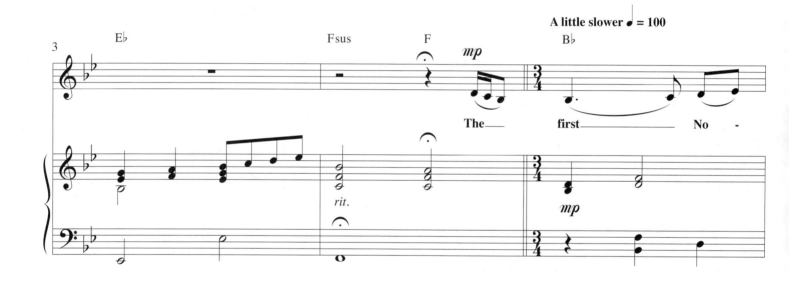

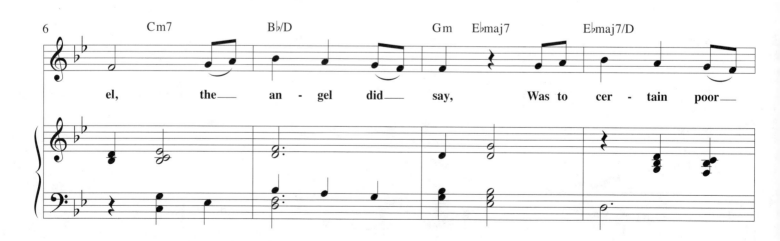

EVEN IF YOU POSSESS A **CCLI** LICENSE YOU CANNOT COPY ANY MUSIC FROM THIS BOOK.
If you have questions about CCLI, please call 800/234-2446.

Do You Hear What I Hear?

Recorded by FFH

**Words and Music by
NOEL REGNEY and
GLORIA SHAYNE**

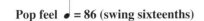

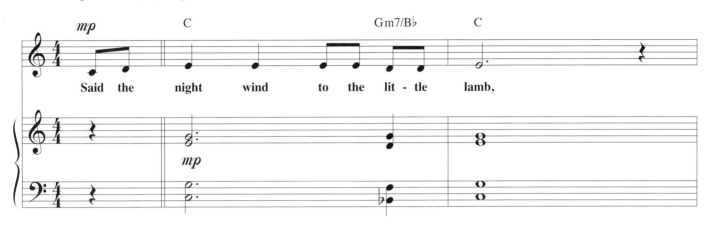

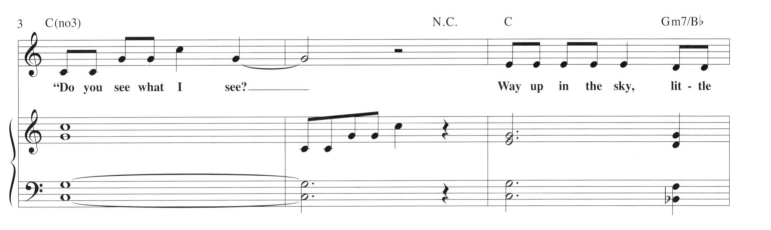

Said the king to the peo - ple ev - 'ry -

Sleigh Ride
with
Let It Snow, Let It Snow, Let It Snow
Recorded by Jump 5

"Sleigh Ride" — Mitchell Parish and Leroy Anderson

232

2nd time to CODA ⊕

31 Am7 · Gm7 · Dm7 · Am/C

love - ly weath-er for a sleigh ride to-geth-er with_____ you. It's

33 Am7 · Gm7 · Dm7 · Am/C

love - ly weath-er for a sleigh ride to-geth-er with_____ you._____ Let it snow!_____

35 Am7 · Gm7 · Dm7 · Am/C

_____ Let it snow!_____ Let it snow!_____ There's a

37 F2 · Fmaj7

birth - day par - ty at the home of Farm - er Gray, it - 'll

love - ly weath - er_____ for a sleigh_____ ride._____

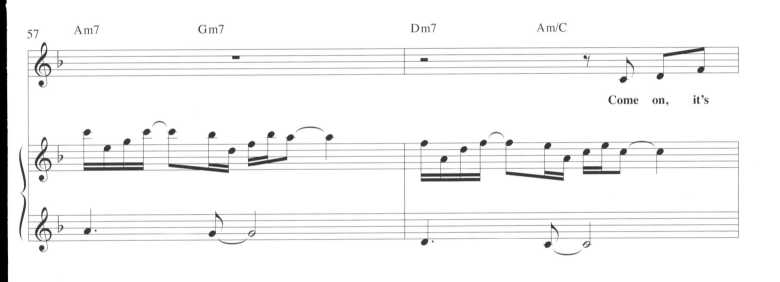

Come on, it's

love - ly weath - er for a sleigh ride to - geth - er with_____ you._____

OTHER ARTIST RELATED
FOLIOS

The following songs are also available in the artist folios listed:

THE CHRISTMAS SHOES (NEWSONG)

Available in the songbook "The Christmas Shoes"

Brentwood-Benson Music Publishing (4575705837)

A CHRISTMAS TO REMEMBER (AMY GRANT)

Available in the songbook "A Christmas to Remember"

Word Music (080689 351280)

DON'T SAVE IT ALL FOR CHRISTMAS DAY (AVALON)

Available in the songbook "Joy"

Hal Leonard (HL00306379)

I'LL BE HOME FOR CHRISTMAS (JACI VELASQUEZ)

Available in the songbook "Christmas"

Word Music (080689 412288)

JINGLE BELL ROCK (POINT OF GRACE)

Available in the songbook "A Christmas Story"

Word Music (080689 349287)

O LITTLE TOWN OF BETHLEHEM (STEVEN CURTIS CHAPMAN)

Available in the songbook "All I Really Want for Christmas"

Hal Leonard (HL00306742)

SILENT NIGHT (SELAH)

Available in the songbook "Rose of Bethlehem"

Word Music (080689 439285)

WOW RECORDINGS & SONGBOOKS

Currently Available from the WOW Series

WOW WORSHIP (AQUA)
CD: Provident Records
(8306108142)
Songbook: Word Music
(080689511288)

WOW WORSHIP (RED)
CD: Word Records
(080688630041)
Songbook: Word Music
(080689472282)

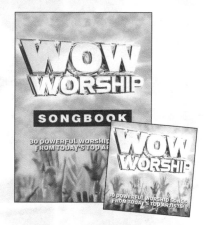

WOW WORSHIP
(YELLOW)
CD: Verity Records (8441801982)
*Songbook: Brentwood-Benson
Music Publishing (4575708397)*

WOW WORSHIP (GREEN)
CD: Integrity Music (000768195567)
Cassette: (000768195543)
Songbook: Integrity Music
(000768195567)

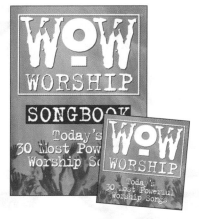

WOW WORSHIP (ORANGE)
CD: Integrity Music (000768172322)
Cassette: (000768172346)
Songbook: Integrity Music
(00076817260)

WOW GOSPEL 2006
CD: Verity Records
(828767516028)
Songbook: Word Music
(080689510281)

WOW GOSPEL 2005
CD: Verity Records
(828766524420)
*Songbook: Brentwood-Benson
Music Publishing
(45757710727)*

WOW GOSPEL 2004
CD: Verity Records
(828765749428)
*Songbook: Brentwood-Benson
Music Publishing
(4575709347)*

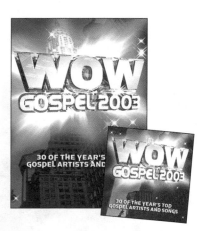

WOW GOSPEL 2003
CD: Verity Records
(012414321329)
*Songbook: Brentwood-Benson
Music Publishing
(4575708287)*

WOW RECORDINGS & SONGBOOKS

Currently Available from the WOW Series

WOW GOSPEL 2002
CD: Verity Records (001241318824)
Songbook: Brentwood-Benson
Music Publishing
(4575706837)

WOW GOSPEL 2001
CD: Verity Records (001241316325)
Songbook: Brentwood-Benson
Music Publishing
(4575704957)

WOW GOSPEL 2000
CD: Verity Records (001241316325)
Songbook: Brentwood-Benson
Music Publishing
(4575703867)

WOW GOSPEL 1999
CD: Verity Records (012414312525)
Songbook: Brentwood-Benson
Music Publishing
(4575703347)

WOW GOSPEL 1998
CD: Verity Records (012414310925)
Songbook: Brentwood-Benson
Music Publishing
(4575703337)

WOW CHRISTMAS
(GREEN)
CD: Word Entertainment (0806886414)
Songbook: Word Music
(080689498282)

WOW CHRISTMAS (RED)
CD: Word Entertainment
(080688607821)
Songbook: Word Music
(080689442285)

WOW THE 90s
CD: Word Entertainment
(080688580728)
Songbook: Word Music
(080689382284)

WOW Gold
CD: Provident Music Group
(8306105332)
Songbook: Brentwood-Benson
Music Publishing
(4575703857)